Trevor Wye

A Beginner's Book for the Flute

Piano Accompaniment

Order No: NOV 120586

NOVELLO PUBLISHING LIMITED

Cover by Art and Design

For Kate Hill

PREFACE

Any new book appearing on the market usually boasts of new ideas and new format. This book is no different in this respect though it does incorporate all the well-tried recipes of the past.

Technically, the flute is the easiest of the woodwind instruments and one which lends itself most readily to being learnt chromatically. It is easier for a beginner to play in different keys, provided that the learning of each new note is given equal emphasis.

The general outline of this book is, therefore, to encourage:
   (a) enjoyment of flute playing and music making in the broadest sense.
   (b) familiarity with the lesser-known keys which, in turn, results in easier access to orchestras and ensembles.
   (c) the formation of a firm low register, the foundation to a good tone throughout the compass of the flute.
   (d) solo and ensemble playing.

The 72 numbered pieces (1-42 are in PART I, the rest in PART II) in this book can mostly be played either:
   1) as a solo
   2) as a duet
   3) as a solo with piano
   4) as a duet with piano
   5) as a solo or duet with guitar accompaniment.

The book of piano accompaniments, in which chord symbols are given, are up to Grade VI (Associated Board) in standard (though many are easier), and is available separately.

The book is intended for both individual and group tuition. It can be used without a teacher if circumstances make this necessary though a pupil is strongly advised to consult a good teacher.

Many exercises and tunes are by the author.

Piano accompaniments by Robert Scott with nine original pieces specially composed by Alan Ridout.

Finally, I acknowledge with grateful thanks, the players and teachers who have advised me on the preparation of this book:

Lucy Cartledge, Catharine Hill, Malcolm Pollack, Rosemary Rathbone, Alastair Roberts, Lenore Smith, Robin Soldan, Hilary Taggart, Stephanie Tromans, Lindsay Winfield-Chislett and Janet Way.

TREVOR WYE

Also available from Novello:

A Practice Book for the Flute by Trevor Wye

This highly successful series of Practice Books for the Flute has proved to be of tremendous value to players of all grades from beginners to advanced students. Each book has a dependence upon the others and concentrates on an individual facet of flute playing in detail. Collectively they form a broad reference to the technical difficulties of the instrument, without concentrating on any one particular method of study.

The six volumes deal with:
    Volume 1   TONE
    Volume 2   TECHNIQUE
    Volume 3   ARTICULATION
    Volume 4   INTONATION AND VIBRATO
    Volume 5   BREATHING AND SCALES
    Volume 6   ADVANCED PRACTICE

SAD TUNE

ALAN RIDOUT

AIR DE BUFFONS

16th century

2 Moderato (at a moderate speed)

DANCE

SUSATO

3 Allegro (quickly)

MADRIGAL

4

THE NIGHTINGALE

FOLKSONG

THE BEE

19th century

LULLABY

ALAN RIDOUT

THE CUCKOO

ANONYMOUS
?19th century

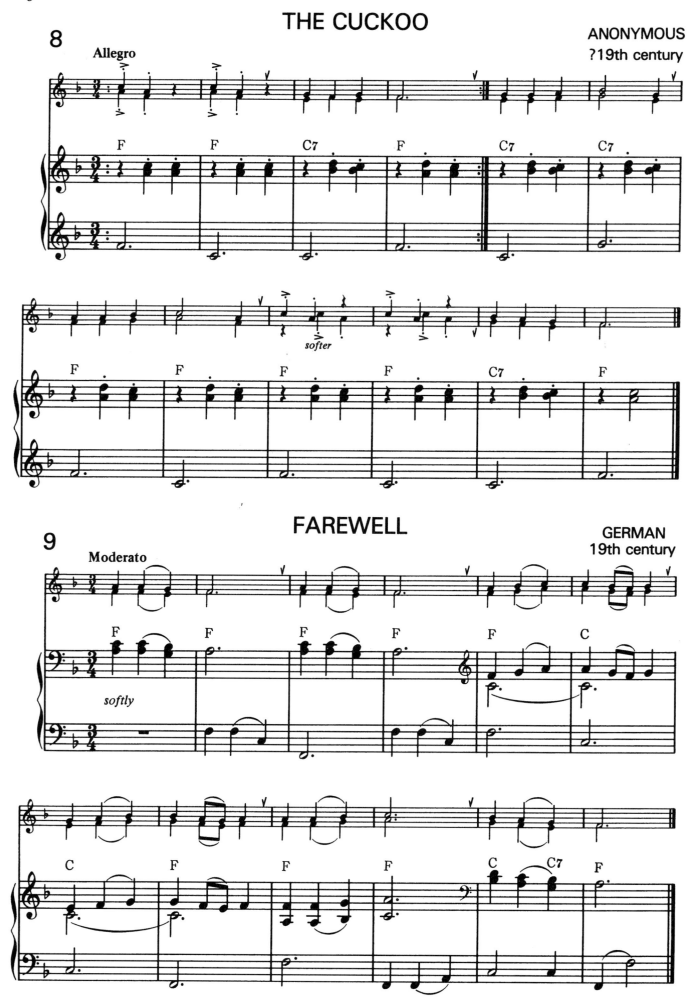

FAREWELL

GERMAN
19th century

DANCE

PRAETORIUS

MELODY

LULLY

MELODY

LULLY

RUSTIC DANCE

ALAN RIDOUT

THE MAIDEN

14

SAD WALTZ

18th century

15

THIS OLD MAN

16

A DANCE

A DANCE

PRAETORIUS

18

AIR

ALAN RIDOUT

19

BRANSLE

GERVAISE

NOEL: *A CANON*

CHEDEVILLE

GERMAN DANCE

MELCHIOR FRANCK

22 Maestoso(majestically)

SWEDISH FOLK SONG

DUDLEY'S GRUNT

18

GERMAN DANCE

SCHUBERT

FOLK TUNE

ALAN RIDOUT

26 Con moto (with motion)

COVENTRY CAROL

Melody arranged by
MARTIN SHAW

27 Lento con moto (slowly with motion)

Melody reprinted by permission of A.R. Mowbray & Co.Ltd.

ALLEMANDE

GERVAISE

LORD HAYE'S MASQUE

CAMPION

OLD FRENCH CAROL

TRADITIONAL

22

RUSSIAN FOLK SONG

WITCHES' DANCE

RONDO

SUSATO

33

O LITTLE ONE SWEET

34

17th century

RONDO

35

SUSATO

MARCH

MELCHIOR FRANCK

MAYPOLE DANCE

GREENSLEEVES

RIGADOON

H. PURCELL

39

DING DONG! MERRILY ON HIGH

FRENCH
16th century

40

TAMBOURIN

RAMEAU

41

BRANLE

42

GERVAISE

THE AQUARIUM

43

SAINT-SAENS

THE ACROBAT

44

A VERY SAD TUNE

HYMN

J. PARRY

MARCH

ALAN RIDOUT

34

SOEUR MONIQUE

48

COUPERIN

PLAISIR D'AMOUR

49

MARTINI

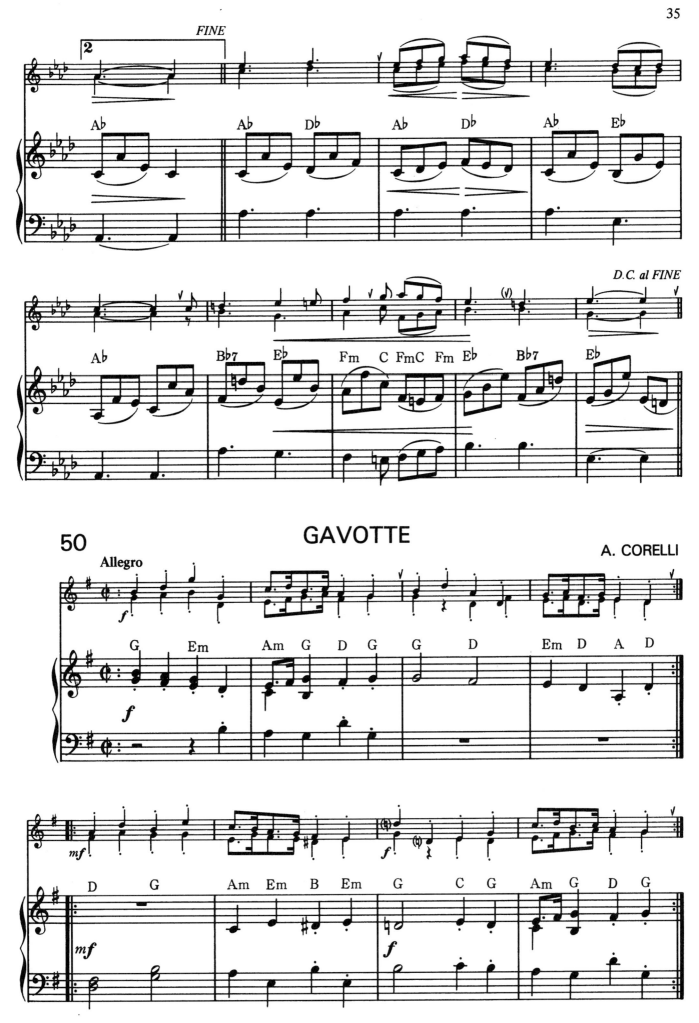

GAVOTTE

50

A. CORELLI

FANTASY PIECE

SCHUMANN

51

52

THE HARVESTERS

COUPERIN

LAMENT

53

ALAN RIDOUT

DANCE

V. HAUPTMANN

40

MINUET

55

J. S. BACH

BALLET

RAMEAU

56

BASS DANCE

ARBEAU-WARLOCK

57

SCOTCH DANCE

BEETHOVEN

MILONGA

SOUTH AMERICAN

NEAPOLITAN AIR

ANONYMOUS
19th century

60 Andantino con moto ♪=132

ANDANTE

ALAN RIDOUT

SICILIENNE

VIVALDI

62

QUEM PASTORES

GERMAN
14th century

Grazioso ♩=108

63

ROSAMUNDE

SCHUBERT

ANDANTE

SCHUBERT

AIR

66 Moderato ♪=112

J. CLINTON

52

LANE'S TUNE

67 PLAYFORD (1695)

BARCAROLLE

ALAN RIDOUT

68

MINUET

J.S. BACH

PIEDS EN L'AIR

70

Andante ♪=112

ARBEAU-WARLOCK

RIGADON

RAMEAU

71

GRAND FINALE
MINUET WITH VARIATIONS

J.J. QUANTZ
freely arranged by T.W.

THEME

Allegro ♩=104

VARIATION I

VARIATION II

VARIATION III

VARIATION IV

62

VARIATION V

VARIATION VI

VARIATION VII